Stream Smarter

170+ tricks Successful Streamers Use To Get More Viewers And
Followers Streaming Games on Twitch

by Max Wegner

www.streamingmentality.com

Disclaimer

This book and the information contained therein are intended for informational purposes only. This book is neither supported nor endorsed by Twitch and is based on the author's opinion, experience and research.

This book contains products, resources and services represented by third parties. The author does not assume responsibility or liability and does not guarantee of any information, opinion or instruction for any Third Party material published in this book.

No part of this book can be reproduced, transmitted, or sold in whole or in part in any form, without the prior written consent of the author. All trademarks in this book are the property of their respective owners.

By using this book you agree that the author is not responsible for the success or failure of your business venture based off the information published in this book.

Your Free Bonus

As a small token of gratitude for you buying this book, I'd like to offer a free bonus gift. This small PDF guide is called:

"10 Easy Steps To A Professional Twitch Overlay for FREE!"

In this PDF guide you'll learn how you can get a professionally designed overlay, logo and other custom graphics for your Twitch channel for FREE!

You can download your FREE gift here:

www.streamingmentality.com/stream-smarter

Table of Contents

Introduction

If you want to start a Twitch channel – start today,

you'll never be ready.

So, you might be new to live streaming on Twitch.tv, but you've heard about people earning fame and fortune playing their favorite video games in front of a camera. Or maybe, you are a seasoned streaming veteran looking to take your Twitch channel to the next level.

Either way, this book is a tool to engineering your success on Twitch. And while it is jam-packed with actionable steps that will have an immediate impact on your channel's stats, it also serves the purpose of giving you food for thought and changing your mentality in the long-term.

This book should be your everyday or at least a once in a while read: always be checking if you could be doing more than you're already doing and whether you are still on the right track. It holds the answers to your questions about how to succeed as a streamer on Twitch, but at the same time I do not claim that this book is the be-all and end-all guide for your streaming life.

I highly encourage you to test the techniques described in this book, do your own research and see what works for you. You need to understand how the Twitch community works and why people come to watch your stream or any stream for that matter.

My goal with this book is for you to be able to create value for your viewers. Your goal in return, is the will to make a difference with your Twitch channel, to do something that is worth doing, having a part in your viewers' lives and transforming your own life. If you are able to create that unique value that only you can provide, people will flock to you to buy that value with their time or money.

It all starts with the mindset of bringing in the **BEST** show on Twitch, no matter if there are 4 people watching or if you're broadcasting in front of a crowd big enough to fill a football stadium. Will you give your 100% every time?

Then read on, you've got what it takes.

Shortcuts to Success as a Streamer

Everybody is looking for the magic bullet and thus I am obligated to mention the shortcuts. There are actually only 3 *realistic* shortcuts to a large Twitch following known to man.

I'm putting an extra emphasis on realistic, because of course there are other ways, but these are rather unlikely (e.g. becoming a viral success with one play overnight) and not really applicable to every person.

Let us have a quick look at what they are:

Shortcut #1: Be good, be really good

And I mean the very top tier good. If you're one of the best players of any game, this is a shortcut to Twitch success. The bigger the community behind the game, the bigger is your potential audience.

High profile League of Legends players and entertainers like **TheOddOne** can carry a stream to victory. A less known, but quite popular competitive game called SpeedRunners has a smaller, but nevertheless loyal fanbase and good players like **Buffet_Time** can build a following with it.

Shortcut #2: Be popular already

Gaining followers becomes so much easier when you've got a prominent face and a solid back-up by rabid fans. You can leverage the fact that people are already following you on other media and Twitch will become just another social place to interact with you.

Leveraging your fans can be done by everyone to some extent: leverage your Facebook, friends and family, as well as communities and forums you're already part of.

Shortcut #3: Be a girl

This one is a no-brainer. Statistically, a female streamer grows much faster than their fellow streamers of the opposite sex. That is despite (or because?) of all the attention and controversy given by feminists and chauvinists alike.

So, if you are a female streamer – read on about how you can accelerate the growth of you channel even more, if you are not – read on and learn how to win more viewers using other tactics.

How to Use This Guide

The resources in this guide are sorted by category. Feel free to start with the category you feel will be most advantageous for you to learn about. This book is simply meant to help you uncover the techniques you need to learn to run a better and a more successful channel on Twitch rather than to follow a narrative.

Some of these tips may be obvious to you, but unknown to other readers. I'm also sure that some of the techniques you've already heard of and you might be using them every day in your Twitch show, but I guarantee, some will be new even to you. There is also a "Bonus" section at the end of a chapter that contains unusual tips.

Some things on this list, like hardware or channel design might seem not as important as other, like promotion and self-marketing. Consider this, though: promoting will get people to your channel, that is true, but the sum of seemingly "unimportant" details, which the hardware might be a part of, is what increases the chances to keep people interested, as well as to make them stay and become loyal followers and viewers.

1. Streaming in general

First, let's talk about the streaming mentality in general, what it means to be broadcasting for other people and all the adjacent factors that contribute to a better user experience. In later chapters we will be discussing the steps you need to take to increase your viewer numbers.

1. ABS: Always Be Streaming

The first one is fairly obvious: every time you stream, there is a chance somebody stumbles over your channel and becomes a follower. While there is a lot behind "simply streaming" and we will get to that later, don't expect to grow quickly if you only stream once a week.

Look at top athletes: Michael Phelps, one of the best swimmers in the world, trains every day for 5-6 hours including Sunday, figuring that this would provide him 52 more days of training per year and an edge over his competitors. Consider this the next time you want to skip a "streaming day".

2. Consistency is key

Many brands, professionals and athletes became a success after doing what they do best for a prolonged period of time. Every time they honed their craft they became better at it and eventually surpassed the training, skills and genetic heritage of their competitors.

Dansgaming started from nothing as a small streamer and kept streaming, building a community of 250,000+ followers over the course of 5+ years by being consistent about what he wants to achieve. If you continue streaming and enjoying it, then trust me - you will be successful.

3. Stream because you enjoy it

"Hey, I'm already playing the game, so I might as well be streaming it on Twitch and the viewers will come." That is the idea of how many of the streamers start their channels, but 99.9% run into a "no viewers" roadblock eventually.

A "streaming to get viewers" attitude isn't too viewer-friendly in itself and simply is not entertaining, neither for you, nor for the viewers. While it is "good enough" to start with, this shouldn't be the driving force behind your ambitions if you really want to GROW your channel.

You do it, because it is fun and you love to stream while entertaining your audience and having a natural banter with the chat.

4. Viewer count is not important

If you are constantly looking at the viewer count, and thinking to yourself that too few or too many people are watching, you change your behavior towards your audience on a subconscious level. And probably not in a better way.

Just keep playing the game no matter how many viewers are watching, do your commentary and give it your best shot.

If the viewer count is high today – good, if it's low tomorrow – there are reasons outside of your reach: people have a Tango Thursday, a Football Monday or are just out of town.

Relax and just keep doing what you normally do. You are not (always) the reason, so don't blame yourself.

5. You are your #1 critic

Watch your VODs and see how you can improve: Talking, gestures, facial expression, chat interaction. Ask yourself these questions:

- Am I happy with my stream?

- Would I watch it?

- What am I doing right?

- What would I change?

And of course follow through with the improvements, don't put them off. If you want to grow, you have to treat your channel like a business and put in the hours. Good enough is a lazy excuse, so you need to always be moving forward. Always strive for the better and work towards it:

- Adding new topics to your show

- Fixing the audio

- Adding more quality visuals, etc.

6. Producing quality content

Streaming an empty chair, tinkering with hardware, performing tests while live on camera, we've seen them all. And most of us do not want to spend their time watching a black screen, when expecting fun and entertainment.

When something happens live – it happens, make the best out of it, but try to reduce these situations to a minimum and perform the necessary testing off-camera.

7. Feedback from friends and family

Don't be afraid to ask friends, family or fellow streamers to watch your stream and to provide constructive feedback. More often than not these people will see something your strained eyes just don't grasp anymore.

8. Sizing up the competition

Oftentimes, to get a better perspective it helps stepping back, and asking: "What do I look for in a new streamer?":

- Do they have a webcam?

- Are they excited or bored with the game?

- Do they respond to the chat?

- Do they have a unique and descriptive graphic overlay, as well as avatar/icons?

- How many viewers/followers?

This makes you realize in which department your own stream is lacking.

9. Facecam: yay or nay?

Many people ask whether they *have* to have a webcam on their stream. A short answer to this question is 'No', a face cam is not a requirement for a good stream to happen. It is rather an enhancement to your show than a must-have.

Streamers seem to do fine without a face cam. But if you're wondering if you SHOULD have a webcam on your Twitch stream, the answer would be definitely 'Yes', you should.

A facecam VASTLY improves your interaction. It allows you to form a stronger and a more emotional connection with people, and as a result they might be more tempted to come back.

A lot of your communication is nonverbal, therefore seeing a streamer, watching the reactions, the emotional rollercoaster during an interesting match, putting a face to the voice, etc. is in fact priceless.

If you think you don't have the face or the physique for a camera – think again. The media is full of extremely successful characters that defy the modern standards of the way one should look or behave on camera. Steve Buscemi, anyone? Some streamers even openly claim being ugly, be it the truth or not.

In conclusion, not having a camera would cripple your channel's growth and you should be aware of that.

10. Always be on the edge, engaged and in the zone, having fun

The first impression is what really counts for new people coming to your channel; and it still sounds true for regulars as well.

Imagine watching a stream or any other show or match on the Internet or TV, where the anchorman is just bored out of his mind with what is currently happening on his screen. Now, that doesn't sound too exciting, doesn't it? Neither is it for the crowd that is supposed to watch it and have fun.

It doesn't really make much sense for you to be playing a boring game or just show your viewers on the stream that you are very tired.

11. Have a schedule and stick to it!

I can't stress enough how important it is to stream regularly and grow anticipation for your stream. Your loyal fan base will know that no matter what, they can count on quality entertainment on certain days.

Treat your stream like how a television network treats its shows. Imagine that your favorite TV show would go live at random times. Or if HBO would schedule Game of Thrones on Sunday every week and then switched the days randomly or miss out on a few dates as the show goes on.

There is no difference between a TV show and your show on Twitch in terms of a schedule. If you stick to a schedule, people will know when to look for you and get excited about new shows. If you don't, your fans will stop showing up eventually.

2. Your Unique Streaming Proposition (USP)

What *makes* your channel or in other words: what is so special about it that people come to your channel to watch it? The obvious answer to this question is: YOU!

But who *are* you and what *makes* you? What is so special about your personality, your channel and your games that people should watch you play?

12. What is your niche?

Pick a niche that people will recognize you by:

- Pro-Gamer: the one with the highest score and the highest rank.

- Helpful advisor: jam packed with wisdom and neat tricks.

- Explaining/Analyzing the plot: happy to invest the extra time to immerse in the story

- Indie: discovering these hidden gems

- Retro: My name is Zelda of Mushroom Kingdom 8bit

- Challenges: games are too easy, let's step it up a little, shall we?

- One Game one guy/girl: Monogamy is a choice!

- Speedruns: Skyrim in less than one hour? The bet is on!

- Looks: **Ms_Vixen** looks good on camera and happens to be a great CoD World at War player as well.

- …

- Your niche?

13. Make every streaming session unique

Is it Christmas? Dress up like Santa and gift giveaways to your viewers. Is it St. Patty's Day? Do the leprechaun dance!

14. Show off your non gaming skills

Do you have other hobbies besides gaming? Music, drawing, deviant art are activities people can relate to.

15. Care about your audience

If you make it about your audience and not about you, providing value that no other streamer can provide at this point you will see your viewer and follower numbers grow. This can be information about the game, insider facts, geek talk, lore, etc.

16. Be different – be remarkable

Do what you want to do: if it's playing indie games – that's fine, finding the longest jumps in Saint's Row – that's fine also; but don't think that you *should* be doing indie let's plays, because it's a thing these days or because streamer X is doing it. Find your own schtick.

3. The Chat

The chat on Twitch is the single most powerful tool to interact and connect with your viewers while you're live on stream. People come into the chat to socialize with like-minded people and to be able to talk to their favorite streamer.

In 9 out of 10 cases neglecting the chat completely is not a good idea. Chats of popular streamers have a life of its own, where viewers talk to each other and the moderators answer simple questions and enforce the chat rules.

17. A helping bot hand

Use Nightbot (www.nightbot.tv) or Moobot (www.twitch.moobot.tv) to keep up with your chat. These simple addons allow you to automate chore tasks and make your life easier:

- keeping trolls and spammers at bay,

- allow custom commands for users and mods

- create polls

- create raffles

- general statistics overview

18. Stay away from greeting bots

It is a good idea in theory, but nothing can replace the good old, genuine and friendly "Hello" from the host.

19. Let bots do what bots do

Let your bot make a sound and pop their name on the screen, if somebody follows you or donates. People love seeing and hearing their names AND they also love knowing that other people hear and see their name on your screen as well.

This gives them a sense of participation and accomplishment, making sure that you, as a broadcaster, notice them.

20. Acknowledge everyone and every donation

People love to be recognized! Tools like twitchalerts.com let you easily set up the alerts for donations. The service is free to use except for keeping 1% of donations.

21. Give some shouts

A simple "Hi Bilbob95, thanks for checking out the stream." might make the difference for a visitor to be staying or leaving. Shout the names of people who:

- follow,

- enter,

- ask you questions,

- donate,

- subscribe.

22. Prepare chat topics

Have a list of questions in your head to ask new people coming in. Things about the game, whether they have their own Twitch channel, what do they play, etc.

Make it about the viewers, what is interesting for them to talk about while watching your stream, rather than telling the story of YOUR life without being asked.

23. Let chat lurkers lurk

Some people just want to watch a game passively, so if you hardly get any response after a few tries, just let them enjoy the show – it just gets more awkward if you insist on engaging them. No one likes to be forced to chat with you.

The best way to handle this is just to move on and keep doing what you are doing – playing the game, doing the commentary and having fun.

24. Grab and keep people's attention

Give newcomers something to do after they stumbled over your channel:

- Song request: www.nightbot.tv can help you with that. People love hearing THEIR song in the stream. Secret sauce: sing along with the song if you like it!

- Voting on a poll, etc.

25. Background music

There is no right or wrong with choosing the background music: some viewers come exclusively because of the music you play, some will give it a miss because of it.

Be sure that you have the rights for playing the music and it is not copyrighted by DMCA, GEMA, etc. Twitch is also adding to its own music library for use in live streams and vods: music.twitch.tv

26. Events for following

Sing the follower song, dress in a Halloween costume, do something crazy and let your followers vote on what you do:

- **ShannaNina** plays her guitar;

- **BroBQ** does ten pushups for every new follower gaining over 800 followers in 2 months.

Make sure you announce what you do in your streaming title and/or channel description. Giving new followers a special treatment can also result in unwilling but funny accidents which can go viral and boost your channel (checkout #polefail on youtube by **SilentSentry**).

27. Greet returning viewers

If people are coming back, you are probably doing something right and they're probably kind of fond of you. Return the favor and acknowledge the fact that you recognize their screen names. Especially if you remember parts of a previous discussion, you might want to bring it up again.

For example if a viewer mentioned having an exam the other day – ask him about how it went. Because that is what you would ask a person you care about. Those little things go a long way towards building a sense of a community.

28. Ask your regular viewers some questions

This can be some pretty mundane things: how was your day, how is your job, what game are you currently playing. As you will get to know your regulars, better conversation topics will come naturally and you'll start treating them as your friends rather than "just" viewers.

It is also an easy way to figure out where your stream is lacking. From technical issues to content requests. Ask you viewers what they would like to see: a challenge, a walkthrough of a new game, a movie analysis, playing with the community or an ARAM session.

29. Regular viewers are the backbone of your army

Build up a core viewership for your show. You want to have people on your channel who

- do not miss an opportunity to watch your streams

- engage in chat

- are just nice folks to have around

These people are particularly valuable to your streaming life. They will become your friends, they won't let your chat fall asleep and they will keep bringing back other viewers.

30. Again, give those regulars a special care

Your focus is not growing a high number of passerby viewers, but a high number of people who come to watch your stream every time it is on air.

Passerby viewers come and go, but it is these regulars that walk the extra mile for you, watch your videos on every channel and promote your content out of their own will. Show them that you care and you'll find yourself enjoying the conversations and the bonds that are forming out of it.

31. Get your chat talking

Encourage your moderators and people viewing your content to say hello to new visitors and answer questions about the game and anything else.

32. Spark a discussion

Ask on-topic questions in the chat that need more than a simple yes or no answer. These questions usually start with:

- Who?

- What?

- Where?

- When?

- Why?

- How?

Once the initial shyness is gone, you can capitalize on the conversation's momentum and join the talking and/or react to the subjects that come up.

33. Actually *ASK* people to follow your stream

One of the biggest mistakes I see is when a streamer is conversing with the chat and everybody is having a good time and the streamer doesn't ask the newcomers to follow the channel. The stream ends, the viewers leave and there is no immediate net gain for the streamer.

Don't be shy to ask your viewers to follow the channel if they're enjoying it!

34. Stay cool

Wait for a question to pop up in your own chat window - don't stop your gameplay to type an answer in the chat. Most people on Twitch are familiar and OK with the 30sec delay between chat input and output on your screen.

Use mods to keep up with greeting, introducing people to the stream. Your friends can take on this role when you're just starting out.

35. Everyone likes to talk about themselves

Some of your viewers that come to chat with you will have a Twitch channel as well. Ask them about their experience and allow a little self-promotion so long as it adds to the overall vibe and stays somewhat on topic.

36. Involve your viewers

Make them part of what is happening on the stream asking them to:

- vote on polls,

- participate in your surveys,

- win giveaways,

- play games with you,

- and by providing them with other, non-stream activities.

37. Share your audience

Do a friendly raid on another streamer – let them know you are there. This is how it works:

1. Shortly before you finish your stream, you choose a channel to raid or take suggestions from the chat. Usually, that should be a channel of a similar or smaller size that plays the same game or a game from a similar genre.

2. You tell your streamers what to say in the raided chat (like "XxX-Streamer sends his greetings" and

post a link to the channel. It's hilarious how streamers react to such unexpected courtesy.

The point? Sharing the love and growing the community, earning gratitude, making friends among other streamers and be an overall nice person to have around.

38. Twitch-surf other channels

Comment on their gameplay and have fun in the meantime.

Bonus

39. Set up "highlight words" to keep up with the chat

When somebody writes a particular keyword in the chat, it gets highlighted. Your keywords could be: your Twitch name, hey, hi, hello, sup, yo, later, gtg, bb, bye, goodbye, game and s.o.

40. Be active on other people's chats

Don't necessarily go in looking to grow your channel, but to enjoy the stream and make new acquaintances. Be helpful and establish a name in your community. It all takes time, but you are here for the long run anyway, right?

4. You as a Streamer

Most people who are joining your stream will come to check out the gameplay. But guess what? They will STAY because of you. Because YOU are playing this game and making a good show out of it. Because you are a good entertainer or a Pro at this game, or maybe even both. Because there is no one like you out there.

Are you ready to share your life with the world? You will become your own trademark that your viewers won't get enough of. There is a market for every personality possible: quiet, loud, proud types of people and everything in between.

But you have to have a personality to begin with.

41. Be yourself

Being silly, friendly, outgoing, and just simply looking like you are enjoying yourself will get you regular viewers. If you're genuinely frustrated and negative, your viewer numbers will plummet. If being grumpy is your thing, make sure it carries entertainment value, nobody likes being around a whiny old horse.

Being yourself is important and you'll find your very *own* fanbase out there. Hardly anybody needs another **Towelliee** or **ManVsGame**, but the streaming world is desperately in need of new, fresh and exciting personalities like yours.

42. Be authentic

ZileanOP has received a ban for pretending to be disabled, when someday he suddenly stood up from his wheelchair and walked out of the room. It is very hard to come back from that. Pretending to be somebody you are not is *not* a sustainable strategy.

43. Do care about your tribe, don't see them as a tool

And IF you say that you care about people, then show it in your behavior, not only your words. There are not many streamers that truly care about people, so interact with your viewership in a meaningful way and make a difference.

44. Be honest and open to discussion

MissMiaRose, previously an actress in adult movies and a streamer today, is shockingly open about her former profession at times. Her fans appreciate her answering questions and sharing her experiences with the chat, while watching her playing games at the same time.

45. Make yourself approachable and vulnerable

Embrace your flaws and share some little-known facts: tell your viewers about this one time at band camp. Gross, yes, but also funny and human.

46. Every single minute is an opportunity rather than a chore

There is "boring work" involved, besides simply playing the game, but look into how every task brings you closer to reaching your goals or teaches you a particular skill that will be useful later. These skills could be:

- Gaming (obviously) – as you become a better player

- Small Talk and socializing – a very useful skill in everyday life

- Analysis – speaking your mind while analyzing puzzle/boss/player patterns

- Networking – bigger network means bigger opportunities

- Etc.

47. Learn from your mistakes

You will make mistakes as you venture forward into streaming. As in real life you will do things that you are going to regret later. Not answering that fan e-mail immediately, losing a business opportunity because of fear, and s.o.

It is important that you understand the mistakes you made, draw your conclusions and not make the same mistake again. Life is all about trying something out, sometimes winning and sometimes failing, but always be learning.

48. Leaders are Readers

Read fiction, non-fiction, blogs, news and s.o. This will be your distinctive advantage, because:

1. You will have much more differentiated topics to talk about and every episode won't be a carbon copy of the previous one in terms of topics.

2. You will enrich your speech with new vocabulary.

3. You will have another hobby.

Every single problem you've ever had in your life has already been uncovered, analyzed and provided with an action plan to solve it. Everything you'll ever need to know or learn to make your own conclusions has already been written. Be a reader.

49. Be healthy

There is nothing wrong with being yourself, but there is nothing wrong with having a healthy lifestyle either. It will help you to feel better, be more energetic and spark it over to your viewers.

50. Show off your good looks

Have a look in the mirror and use that comb or mascara! That is especially true for female gamers. Although the gaming universe is mainly populated by men, female gamers need to embrace their gaming nature instead of hiding it.

Instead of fearing sexist jokes, just be ready for them and make your gender your competitive advantage. People come to your channel seeking entertainment and eventually, it is you who is going to decide how to entertain them: be it your skills, your personality or your looks and piquant stories.

51. Wear a colorful outfit

When people are browsing through Twitch's game directory they are looking at the thumbnails. If you wear something that makes you stand out, people are more likely to click! Be careful about transparent materials though.

52. Flashy environment

Having party lights and special effects going off in the background makes your thumbnails look different in comparison to the masses and more attractive to viewers.

53. Have a break

Give yourself a break when you notice fatigue or weariness. It is ok and sometimes even necessary to take a weekend off, go for a walk and do other things besides streaming. Don't forget to let your followers know about the sabbatical.

54. Have fun

If you're not having fun, because you don't like the game, you are tired or for any other reason, it will show. Way too many Twitch partners are simply burning out and not passionate anymore about what they are doing.

Especially if you are just starting out, find a way to make it fun *just for you*. If you are not having fun; then no one is going to watch someone who is clearly not having a good time.

5. Talking

Talk, talk, talk. Why is talking on your stream so important? Because of two basic reasons:

1. **Game commentary**: it allows you to give your opinion on the game and generally to speak your mind.

2. **Chat Interaction**: Being able to respond to your viewers in chat and engaging in meaningful conversations.

And both of these aspects are an important part of a healthy and entertaining show on Twitch.

There are exceptions, of course, like **TSM's Dyrus** playing LoL, who is very calm and rarely talks or even moves. But he is actually good at this game and he is a member of one of the most if not *the* most popular LoL team in the world. He already has skills and fame: 2 out of the 3 shortcuts mentioned at the beginning of this book.

However, let's have a look at how you can improve your talking.

55. Build up the ability to talk all the time

You know how they say that 90% of the success is just "showing up"? In regards of talking it is just "opening your mouth" and saying the first thing that comes to your mind.

It's like having an argument with yourself: making a claim, bringing examples and counter examples and just rolling from there.

Next time when you are playing a game, try to step back and listen to your own thoughts. This is what you should be speaking out loud to your audience.

Some people say that it becomes easier for them if they imagine as if they were talking to a friend while playing the game.

I know it might be weird sometimes to talk at your screen, even if nothing is going on. However, do that for a month straight and you'll have established a flow for yourself.

56. What to say

Speaking is a muscle that can be trained if used frequently. Here are some ideas what to talk about when streaming.

1. Internal dialogue

Speak out loud every thought that comes across your mind; e.g. when you think: "We really need to kill this boss so I can upgrade my gear" – just say it and take it from there. You're your commentary on the situation, your concerns, thoughts, as well just rambling about the game and life in general.

Dansgaming made it his boon interacting with the game directly, like talking at the NPCs that mean harm to his player character.

2. Explain

Similar to the internal dialogue, but more about the game – story, lore, gameplay, mechanics. A good example is **TrumpSC**, a Hearthstone player who isn't necessarily THE best Hearthstone player, but he takes his time to explain his every single step in the game.

3. Entertain

If you're a funny guy or girl – crack a joke and have a good laugh with your audience! Tell relevant stories from the (gaming) industry. If you bring something to the game and entertain your viewers, you don't have to be the best of the best. **Markiplier** isn't the best player in the world, but the entertainment part is enormous.

You can mention pop-cultural references, give your opinion on news in the world of games, stars, music, movies, etc. In fact, you can base a whole show around talking about music while playing video games. Try it out! People love **Northernlion's** semi-erudite talk about music, diving deep into 90's and early 2000's.

57. Practice your voice

You can even do it when nobody is watching: 1000 viewers – great! Speak you mind! 0 viewers – great! Practice your commentary! Streamers like **VoiceOfKarnage** make their voice the signature feature of their channel.

58. Move on after a faux pas

If your commentary begins to stutter or a joke has led you nowhere, just move on like nothing happened or admit it with a laugh.

59. You are the host

Imagine that you're hosting a radio show or a podcast and practice different topics. It doesn't hurt having some real friends over or connecting with people via Skype.

Or how about some fictional characters joining your show? People are either hating or loving **PewDiePie**, but you can't deny that his ability to build an imaginary world around him (Stephano, Gonzalo) is remarkable.

60. Connect with your demographic

Ask your viewers questions about their age, occupation, etc. When you know who is actually enjoying your stream, you'll have a much easier time to serve them and yourself a better show, without necessarily twisting around too much.

You can use the free service surveymonkey.com to create a survey and ask your viewers to participate to make the channel better.

61. Are you funny?

If your friends think you're funny, you'll find that your audience will be entertained by your jokes and stories as well.

62. Answering personal questions

Your viewers will want to know you better, so be prepared answering questions about your occupation, your relationships, etc. It's your call whether to crack the door a small amount or burst it open. Hint: people can relate better to you with the latter.

63. Celebrate small victories live

Hit 10 viewers today, reached 100 subscribers, a VOD made 500 views – share your emotions and gratitude with your viewers.

This is essential for motivation: if you see that you are on the right path, making progress, you will be more energetic about your streaming and life in general.

64. Strong language and swearing

Twitch has a "mature content" switch if you're planning your stream to be a one giant F-Bomb. If that's how you talk, the way you are - go for it, you will attract a certain audience that will enjoy it.

Eventually it all boils down to who you are: if you're all about using strong language, there is nothing that should be stopping you from being you and doing so on Twitch.

65. Envy

Neither verbally, nor mentally should you be comparing yourself to other streamers: streamer A has been streaming for 2 years with 10 followers; Streamer B for 2 months with 2,000 followers already: you don't know their goals, you don't know them and the work they did, you don't even know if the follower count is legit (unless you ask the streamer all these things).

There will always be streamers that have more or less success than you, make it your habit to learn from other's successes and mistakes, rather than drowning in self-pity.

6. Dealing with negativity

We all face difficulties and (oftentimes self-made) obstacles in our lives and that includes streaming on Twitch and dealing with negativity or toxic viewers. A toxic community will drain your energy, as well as the energy of your otherwise healthy and happy viewers.

Be humble and relaxed. Instead of having an argument, just shrug and laugh everything off, because toxic behavior on the internet is as certain as death and taxes. So, who cares about one troll venting his anger off? There will always be trolls and haters.

66. Kiss a frog

Sometimes you could befriend a troll and turn them into a "prince" or a "princess", so there is hope for everyone. Don't troll back, unless that is how you handle it, because that helps nobody.

67. The ban hammer

Don't be afraid to show the ban hammer to instill order and keep the viewership safe from trolls and angry internet jerks. You don't even have to say anything to them. Just block them and don't even dwell on it too much thinking over their behavior and your part in it.

Once you do that, carry on like business as usual. Don't even mention it to the chat. Once you earn some loyal viewers, these viewers will be happy to be your moderators and to take some of the burden off of you. Bots can help to some degree as well.

68. Don't get discouraged by negative comments

People who are just passing by will tell you things you don't want to hear: things about your gameplay, about your looks, that you should quit streaming and so on.

Grow a tough skin and NEVER let it through when people are trying to discourage you from doing what you love. You don't care about opinions of people that want you to take a u-turn on your life's goals and you don't take it as a personal reflection. *Period*.

69. Girl Gamers

If you are a girl gamer, you are going to deal with more attention to your sex; much more than a male gamer would. The same kind of attention you would be getting in a bar, club or when going out.

Sexist comments, criticizing skills, flirtation, biased opinions combined with the anonymity of the web are a big playground for people on the internet.

Get used to it and brush it off your shoulders, setup "banned words" on your channel (Settings > Chat > Banned Words) and make your mods take care of the rest.

Learn from strong and popular female streamers:

- **VeeBunni** - Business owner

- **Livinpink** - a Law graduate

- **TaraBabcock** - Speaker, writer, model and public person on the web

7. Promoting Your Channel

Contrary to popular belief, streaming success on Twitch is not always only about grinding out more streams, producing more content or having the best gear. It is much more about what you do before a streaming session and after it.

99% of people don't know how to build a strong promotion strategy and end up spamming other people's chats and threads with a single "I stream on Twitch, check out my stream!" – this serves nobody.

On the other hand, many streamers think that self-promotion has to be sleazy. Quite the opposite is true: well executed promotion is built upon establishing relationships and a helping mentality; as in: how you can help your audience to have a better time on your show or how you can help other streamers reach *their* goals and gain something from it yourself.

70. For starters

Get support from friends and family: share your stream to all your friends on FB: because, if you have 0 viewers, chances are your show will be buried amongst other streams.

Having friends and family tuning in when you stream will help get your stream ranked higher in the Twitch browse results. This will give you a higher chance of people checking out your stream and a faster organic growth.

71. Twitch Spotlight

If you're a partner, make use of Twitch.tv's own spotlight feature by sending a Twitch PM and explaining your stream in a short video.

72. Twitch teams

Another option for partnered channels is to create a twitch team of fellow streamers to push a brand together and promote each other. If you're not a partner, you can still benefit from a twitch team by joining one!

There are no hard requirements for a streamer for joining a team or many teams. Note: you can manage your team setup via Twitch – Settings – Channels & Videos – Teams.

73. Being active in the community

Be active in your game's community that is focused more around content consumption rather than production, for example:

- mmo-champion.com,

- Steampowered.com,

- Reddit.com

- a game's official forums

If you are able to make a name for yourself and add to your internet fame – it is going to net you proportionally more viewers.

Twitch.tv is both a negative and a positive example of this – the forums contain some valuable information, but are oversaturated with posts "I'm a new streamer and I don't get any views" and alike.

So, when you are looking to become part of a community, don't spam yourself around and make sure to add something valuable to the discussion, before talking about your stream.

74. Create a group in Steam

Create your own Steam-group and add all your friends and followers. Every time you log-in or play something, members of your group will get a notification, e.g. **"Aremis86** is playing DayZ" and might check it out!

75. Contribute to a forum, a blog, a wiki

Literally anything where people come to check out their favorite games, talk about them, do theorycrafting and spend their time, is worth checking out. This might be a general forum about games, a subsection of a big online media production or the blog of your favorite streamer.

The most important thing is, that it needs to cater to a big and active gaming community.

Some general examples are:

- Steampowered.com

- Ign.com

- Gamespot.com

- Kotaku.com

- Twitch.tv: forums, team, group, or sub-network on Twitch

- Wow server sub-forum

Towelliee has spent a lot of time posting on WoW forums to get people involved in his brand and into what he is doing on Twitch.

76. Reddit

Reddit is a huge community of millions of engaged users. It is zealously watched over by moderators and thus keeps the discussion on a productive level.

77. Link your Twitch channel to Reddit

You should link your twitch channel to your reddit profile, so when you post on reddit, people will see your Twitch tag.

78. Contribute to subreddits

The plethora of different subreddits offers a magnificent potential for getting your name out there. Games' subreddits, TIL, TIFU, FUNNY can all be used to start or join a discussion and earn a solid reputation over time, like **FerretBomb** who is an active reddit user.

79. Focus on subreddits relevant to your niche

Choose subreddits and participate in them depending on your game or gaming niche and add value to it.

7.1 Networking with your viewers

Twitch is so much fun when you are capable of getting the admiration and the appreciation of your viewers. Give something back!

80. Befriend your viewers on Social Media

Your viewers will appreciate this gesture and you can invite them to check out your other channels. Similar to your official streaming Facebook account, where they can get all the news about what you are up to.

81. Play with your viewers and followers

Ask your viewers what games they play and chances are (as they happened to stick along) they like the same games as you do. Schedule a gaming session with your viewers and encourage them to share the event on their social media.

Not only do you gain loyalty points with your existing followers that join you in this event, but you also make yourself look approachable to other potential fans.

82. If viewers stream too, shout out their names, visit their channel, schedule games with them

This way they will tap into your audience while you can click into in theirs – that's a win-win type of the situation for both parties involved. Don't be afraid to lose viewers to other streamers, if they want to leave, they will – you can't put shackles on them, so you might as well profit from the free flow of viewers on both sides.

83. Send a "Thank You" message

Viewers will come and go and sometimes there is nothing you can do about it. Well, almost nothing. If you are a small streamer, watch the viewers that visit your channel and send them a "Thank You for dropping by" message after you finish streaming. You can have a canned message ready for this matter.

84. Message viewers that unfollow your channel

You should know the reasons: was it the shift in your content, your commentary, games you play or no reason at all? You might get these people back to your channel and learn a valuable lesson about your audience at the same time.

85. Keep your eggs in different baskets

Never rely on Twitch or any single platform to take care of you and your audience. It is better to give your audience some alternatives beyond your Twitch stream: homepage, YouTube, podcast, etc.

86. Grow some online real estate

Get a website where all the information and channels run together and automate it. Nowadays, it doesn't require lots of skill and dedication, nor lots of money to build a pretty website. For as little as ~$10/month you can run your very own website using Wordpress.

Wordpress plugins such as Automatic Youtube Video Posts Plugin or IFTTT can fully automate your website, updating it with fresh videos from YouTube, embedding your live Twitch stream, your Tweets or news from other Social Media.

The point? Getting that free Google traffic and having a place for your fans to rally in. Another, less apparent point is to grow an asset. If you are familiar with Robert Kiyosaki's "Rich Dad Poor Dad" book series, you will know how important assets are.

These assets will produce long term revenue (monetary and non-monetary), without you even touching them.

87. Go to real life special events

BlizzCon, PAX, etc. offer gamers the chance to connect with game developers, industry influencers and with each other. Being in the know of who is who and clever networking can help to grow your channel.

7.2 Networking with other streamers

Twitch is a social place. You can make friends, join events, interact with other people and share your opinion with everybody on the platform. And guess what, there are other people, streamers, just like you, fighting for attention. Join forces with them.

The **Northernlion** Live Super Show for example, hosts a range of his streamer friends playing games together or just sharing a commentary.

88. Make friends in the industry/niche/game and network with them

This is the time to get social and connect to other like-minded people, be it other streamers, developers, community managers, etc. One of the most important things is to give something to the community first and to be giving 10 times more before asking for something in return.

This technique is thoroughly described in Gary Vaynerchuck's book "Jab, Jab, Jab, Right Hook", which is a worthwhile read, if you're serious about establishing an internet personality.

So before asking influencers about help, make sure to ask yourself this question first: What am I doing to add value to their lives? Am I genuinely trying to make their life easier/better/more entertaining?

89. Make sure to befriend your fellow streamers

This not only helps to grow your channel by opening it to another audience, but you can also learn a lot from other streamers.

90. Help others, share your knowledge

Follow them, give them shouts and advice, share their posts every time they are live. Reciprocity is one of the strongest psychological mechanisms known to man. In simple words it states that if you help somebody, then this person is inclined to give you something in return.

So, if you comment on their threads/tweets/FB posts – they'll probably do the same, especially if your channels are about the same size or if yours is bigger. Drop a hint that you are a streamer as well.

91. Reach out to other streamers

After establishing a (non-spammy) name for yourself, you need to reach out to streamers you like and ask for shout outs, collaborations, etc. Established streamers with "street cred" can vouch for you in their streams and channels.

You don't have to carry out this fight for popularity alone – there are others, just as eager as you and you can help each other! Be mindful of giving at least as much as receiving, with giving being there first, before receiving.

92. Promote others

Give a friendly shout, let others know that you appreciate their work and that they are an inspiration to you as a streamer, promote their channel on your show. Based on the reciprocity principle others will do the same.

93. Giveaway your viewers

Before turning off your stream, giveaway your viewers by suggesting them streams to watch after you finish your stream. This "selfless" act probably won't cost you any loyal viewers, but the viewers AND the fellow streamers will thank you for that.

It helps of course, if you set up an agreement with those fellow streamers, but even if you don't, it's good for your karma.

Bonus

94. Watch other channels

A lot. Get into a habit of scanning and monitoring your community and learning about the latest trends. There is a lot to say about other people's success and what actually makes their stream. What is their secret sauce? What makes people watch their stream regularly?

Always try to reverse engineer their quirks and learn from them. Don't be intimidated by their fame, their cosmic talking skills, hardware set-up, game knowledge or [insert valuable skill here].

Most of them started small, tried things out, experimented, worked hard to acquire these skills and most importantly, they persevered. You are actually in a better position today than they've been years or months ago. You have the time machine in front of you: their YT channel, their Twitch VODs, their Twitter account.

Study your favorite streamers:

- their lives,

- careers,

- what shaped them,

- what has made them the way they are now?

What did they do to get where they are now and how can you replicate the process applying what they did and peppering it up with your own personality?

95. Join forces with a team/network

There are many networks who will take on streamers of any size to mentor them and help expose their stream and grow the network via team play. You can leverage their reputation to add to your own popularity.

Here are some of them:

- pwning.com - is a site where you can discover new streamers and get featured for more exposure by being active in their chats.

- teamliquid.net - all about StarCraft 2 streams

- solomid.net - official website of Team Solo Mid

- rizeupgaming.com - streaming network promoting tolerance, opposing discrimination and prejudice, and creating healthier communities for future gamers.

- team2g.org - a fast growing network of players mainly focused on MOBAs

7.3 Social Media

Social Media Outlets like Facebook, Twitter, YouTube, etc. - USE THEM! Don't be shy about putting your face out there: marketing yourself really helps.

And there is no single perfect channel for self-publishing, because every social media tools rely on different key features and its users expect a differentiated approach.

That's why it won't help much "just" posting a link to your new video on every single platform there is – it's just spammy. It is better to create less, but custom made content for every platform or re-create one single piece of content for different platforms.

Tweet, share, blog, and do all the social media promotion you can, to build up anticipation.

Example: When you start streaming your weekly session of "First Impressions" of a new game, you can do the following on your Social Media channels:

- **Facebook**: One hour before starting you post a link to your twitch channel along with something like "What does the 'D' stand for?" and let your followers guess what the game is going to be.

- **Instagram**: Take a picture of yourself holding the copy of the game and blur out the cover.

- **Twitter**: Post a hint about today's game.

- **Youtube**: After you've done streaming and recording the session, you can render the session with a nice intro and outro and upload it to Youtube. You can also make a Best-Of montage of the session and/or funny moments. Re-post the links to the videos on your other Social Media with catchy titles: "Luckiest drop of my life!"; "Scariest moments"; "PENTAKILL!! (Well, almost…)".

96. Use FB to stir up emotions

Remember your emotions after beating a game or failing at it for the X time? Make a post about it! Take a screenshot, jot down a quick description and post it on FB.

97. Search for local Facebook groups

People that play the same game as you or stream in the same area find themselves looking for a community of like-minded people. Facebook is a good place to start looking! Search for "NY World of Warcraft", "NY MOBA", "NY LoL" etc. and join the groups.

Look into how you can support these locals, doing scrims with them. It is amazing how many people are actually happy to give some love and support to streamers from their vicinity!

98. Twitter

Encourage your viewers to interact with you on Twitter using your personal hashtag. You can use TweetDeck to manage your Twitter account(s) live, allowing you to see everyone who follows, favorites, tweets or re-tweets you. Use the OBS window capture feature to display the program live.

99. Instagram

Instagram is another channel that helps to build a close connection with your fans, heavily relying on visuals. Break it and let your creativity run free showing:

• your taste in fashion,

- places you've been to

- and an occasional food shot.

Check out Markiplier's Instagram for inspiration.

100. Youtube

Post every second of your stream on YouTube: past broadcasts, highlights, podcasts, everything. Make sure to include your twitch channel in the description or in the overlay. YouTube is the second largest search engine on the Internet.

Not only will you grow your brand on a secondary platform (YouTube), but the viewers will come and check out your Twitch channel as well.

The more videos you upload, the greater the chance and the overall value. Twitch.tv makes it very easy to upload your videos directly to YouTube with just a couple of clicks.

101. Steam

Create/join a group and after establishing a name there (naturally after 10 posts or so) reach out to the community telling about your stream.

102. Snapchat and other tools outside of the big players

Snapchat isn't quite established yet, but it's a fun tool to message quick and funny pics and videos. As with all social tools that aren't big yet it might be a good opportunity to join and be one of the pioneers while it grows.

103. Make a meme

Check out COD memes for some inspiration.

104. Branding is important

Make an effort that every platform you are being active on displays your name and matches the color scheme of your main channel. And make sure to stand out!

Bonus

105. Find and participate in Twitter discussions

Tweet relevant stuff using hashtags like @TwitchTVGaming or other appropriate hashtags (game, meme, publisher, developer, etc.). You can engage with people talking about your favorite game and make new friends that weren't watching your videos.

Doing it regularly really sums up and helps you get noticed.

7.4 Special events

Special events are a great opportunity to grow your Twitch channel. Big live events in real life are something that you remember for a long time: watching the Super Bowl, going to a live concert or a basketball game.

There is something special in being part of the event, which transfers nicely into Twitch as well. Hosting a special show will give your viewers a highly emotional sense of being there with you, watching you win or fail, laughing and crying with you.

Live shows can't be edited and what happens live, stays on the internet and helps build up a stronger connection with your viewers.

106. 24-hour marathons

These marathons are a big commitment to your viewers and to the cause you are streaming for. This can be charity, a company event, a "The Elder Scrolls 1-5 Marathon" or just streaming 24 hours for its own sake.

Create a series of promotions for these bigger events:

- Create a YouTube video if you have a YT channel

- Promote it on your 'offline' overlay

- Repeat it to your live viewers

- Every other platform or forum you are active on should know about your endeavor

Lobosjr plays a marathon every time a new "Souls" game (Demon's Souls, Dark Souls, Dark Souls 2) or respective DLCs come out.

With a more recent title called "Bloodborne" he started playing it the second it was officially available on PS4. Then he slept and played again. Up until he finished the game in around 30 hours of play time. And then he started a new playthrough and then a third one.

During this special event he made 100-200 new (re-)subs, gave away 5 copies of the game, as well as Play Station 4 and had a blast just playing the game.

When **OneRandomDolly** did her full 24hr stream, it gave her channel a real boost. She grew to over 100 viewers, over 200 follows every stream since then and was partnered by Twitch.

Consider Patreon and other fundraiser platforms to raise some money that can be reinvested into improving your show and buying giveaways.

107. Pre-release event

When the sequel of a hyped game or an expansion is coming out, the interest for the prequel or the original game sparks anew. Remember how WoW subscribers went up every time a new addon was announced or was close to launch? How the sales for Half-Life increased every time there is a tiny bit of news about Half-Life 3?

Fact is, you can use the hype to host an event, playing through the original game before the sequel is released. Look up the release dates of the games you stream and plan events around those dates. Roll in the marketing before the event begins; prepare giveaways and some coffee.

108. Cross-stream event, dual streaming, community face-off, co-op

By establishing yourself in the Twitch community and getting to know other streamers you can approach them to set up a collaborative event. This will effectively grow your channels, with both of you enjoying the social experience.

Samples:

- Live raiding/PvPing in WoW with other streamers

- Starting the same single player game simultaneously

- MOBAing

It works best with channels of similar sizes, but you won't get killed for asking a more prominent streamer! Just make sure you provide value to his channel up front as well. Believe in co-opetition: there is enough pie for everyone.

109. Q&A event

Connecting with your viewers regularly by putting a session of Q&A with your viewers into your schedule makes your bond with your fans stronger. **Nobbel87** hosts a regular live Q&A with his followers on all things WoW.

Make a weekly podcast, a daily intro/outro of Q&A on every stream, a monthly round ups with other Twitch streamers, etc. Learn to keep it consistent.

110. Celebrity bonus

Get a developer of a game or somebody from the industry exclusively on your channel and promote the hell out of this event on the respective platforms and forums. Make sure you encourage the celeb to do so as well.

It is easier than it sounds: especially Indie-developers will be happy to speak about and get more eyeballs onto their game.

Bonus

111. Ask people to spread the love

During your live event, ask people that are watching to share your stream! Social Media, Twitter work quite well. Don't be shy about asking what you want, you are the entertainer and people watching are obviously enjoying the show, so why not spread the word about the good stuff?

You'll be amazed about the results.

112. In-game events

Host or join raids in MMORPGs, tournaments in FPS, MOBAs and RTSs, competitive games, as well as multiplayer games in general and don't forget to tell participants that they're live on your stream!

7.5 Giveaways

Streamers usually use giveaways to show their gratitude to their viewers and of course to get new viewers on board.

113. Giveaways for joining

Giving away stuff to people that join your channel is what you can do to get more viewers that stick around. This is especially effective when you're new to give yourself a chance to emerge from the bottom of the Twitch game directory.

Don't forget to find a corresponding title: "First day in H1Z1 – Giveaways for joining!"

114. Giveaways for staying around

Prepare an appropriate title for your stream, such as "Playing with subs - Game Y Giveaway after every boss". People will come for the giveaway and stay for the stream. Humble Bundle, Indie Gala, etc. are great platforms to stock up on for giveaways.

Gaming houses and streamers like **Swifty**, who actually owns a gaming house take it to the extreme and leave the cam on 24/7 whether they're streaming or not. Users earn points for being on the channel that they can bid to win games and gear.

8. Selecting your games

Honestly, there is not one game out there that is guaranteed to raise your views on a consistent basis. Any game you can play out there is being played by someone else. Possibly to a few thousand viewers. There is no such thing as the best game to stream.

But there are games that are more advantageous to net you more viewers.

115. Play the games you enjoy

In general, it might sound cheesy, but if you enjoy playing the game, your viewers are more likely to feel that vibe, and both you and your viewers will have a good time.

On the other hand, if you force yourself playing a popular game which you think is boring as sin, you will not only waste your own time which you could spend playing something fun, but also the time of your viewers. Because, if you don't find the game interesting, the content you produce probably won't be interesting.

"Stream what you love" is such a universally good advice because you won't get tired of it and you are much more likely to eventually get viewers that stick around.

Northernlion has over 1.000 episodes of "The Binding of Isaac" on YouTube alone, not counting in the episodes that were available on Twitch only or his gameplay off camera. He loves the game and produces content for it on a daily basis. If he wouldn't stream it, he'd still be playing it.

116. On the other hand: ENJOY the games you play

If that's only to grab the opportunity and to ride on the hype that a game is getting at a particular point. This hype could be: a release of a major title (Call of Duty franchise), an expansion (Hearthstone/WoW), major gaming events (LoL tournaments) and other events that can bring a classic game back to light (#AGDQ2015).

You can have some fun with it while it's still fresh, make your coverage, tell your opinion and put it back on the shelf. And who knows, you might even discover a whole new genre for yourself.

117. You want to become a better player

Choosing a competitive game like LoL, Starcraft 2 or DotA 2 for the sake of gaining a followership makes more sense if you're good at it or have the desire to become a good player.

118. You are a top player

If you're good at a particular game and enjoy it – stream it! Watching a game you win at, is more fun to watch than a game you fail at over and over. This also means that improving your skill at a game will reward you with viewers in the long term.

With the rise of competitive gaming and streaming, pro players begin to gain the status of a celebrity. Top players from LoL, DoTA 2, CS, StarCraft 2 and Hearthstone pretty much own a lion's share of Twitch's total viewers.

119. Build a portfolio

You might want to build up a portfolio streaming different games that you like, tapping into different viewerships and see how you viewers react.

120. Become the go-to guy or girl for a game or a range of games

Check out Northernlion for "The Binding of Isaac" as an example. He plays lots of games, but you can always come back to his channel for a round of Isaac from time to time.

Other examples: **ThunderCast** and **Lobosjr** with Dark Souls, **Bananasaurus_Rex** with Spelunky, or **Darkwinge** with FTL. Another example that is a bit off, because it is a YouTube channel, but nevertheless shows off what is possible if you focus your efforts is **Vaatividya**.

Vaatividya is a channel on Youtube and he is a go-to, if not THE go-to guy when it comes to Dark Souls Lore. His videos are all about lore of a SINGLE game series, fueled by a great community and Patreon.

121. Play one game exclusively

This is a hard-core approach on the first glance, but there are many streamers that play one game only. And they play it on a really high level or even competitively. **FredFrost**, a virtuous Shaco player in League of Legends, played this single champion only (unless he got banned) and was able to grow a remarkable following doing so.

Playing one game exclusively is great if you just love playing it, and also because you can piggyback other games and genres from it. Your viewer base will happily back you up when you try out new games.

If you want to play something exclusively, but not necessarily a competitive MOBA, FPS or RTS, it should be a game that has a high RNG basis to it. Something that has a different twist every time you play it, so it stays interesting for a long time.

122. Choose a game that has an ACTIVE community

This one is actually very important, meaning that people should still be avidly talking about the game on forums, people are still uploading videos to YouTube and it has a decent viewership on twitch. Announce your streams on the respective forums.

You might want to participate a bit in the discussion first, before coming along as spammy.

123. Play exclusive titles

Having an extremely restricted, pre-launch access to the next big game is a sure-fire way to gain momentum. It is not a viable strategy to building your channel around it, because it is not guaranteed that you have that access all the time.

Networking with influencers, game developers and building relationships with them helps though.

124. Beta access

Being able to play a beta version of a game has a touch of exclusivity as well, however it's not a standalone show anymore. Look for sites that list all games from a particular genre that are in open or close beta phase.

125. Do play on a launch day

Launch day games are a pretty sure shot to gain some attention from people that want to buy or just check out a new game.

126. Early access games on Steam

Scour Early Access and Greenlight on Steam for games that are hyped by press and community.

127. Obscure gems

The market for Indie games is hot with many critically acclaimed games such as Minecraft, The Binding of Isaac, Hotline Miami, FTL, etc. surpassing the sales figures and popularity of AAA-titles for a fraction of developing cost. Grab a copy and be the first one to play it.

128. Creativity pools

Make use of your creative energy in games like Minecraft or Sims and build your own beautiful and unique world.

129. High grade of individuality

Games like Skyrim or MMOs with many optional paths offer every user a unique experience. People might be curious about other storylines, characters or classes they never tried.

130. Games with randomly generated content and sandbox games

DayZ, Rogue Legacy, Binding of Isaac, GTA V Online – every session is different and therefore stays interesting.

131. Linear gameplay and older games

On the other hand you should probably stay away from playing (older) games with a linear story that plays out the same every time. Players who have beaten the game don't need a gameplay reminder and the others might want to play the story themselves. This format is better suited for YouTube where you can upload your playthrough VODs.

However, this isn't true for games with a devoted community where frequent runs are still interesting and watchable for the reasons stated above.

132. Games with high stakes or just difficult games

A game, where the player has something to lose when he or she fails:

- In Dark Souls, the player loses character progress if he is not able to retrieve his souls.

- DayZ forces the player to start the game over if he dies.

- If you lose your party member in "The Darkest Dungeon", the champion stays dead and the time and resources invested are lost as well.

So, in other words, it can build up some tension if you have something to lose that is interesting to watch. Games like the above, roguelikes and hardmodes with permadeath work for this type of USP.

133. Get good on a new game

If you manage to get to the top tier on a new popular game faster than anyone else, you'll have the chance to reap the fame. Choose games that with a longer prognosticated lifespan: MOBAs, MMOs and eSports games.

Smite and Heroes of the Storm are such games, although the MOBA genre is quite saturated with big names, there is still a market share to be gained with these.

134. If you are just starting out

Don't play games which are too popular already, unless you are really good or have the desire to become good. If you play games which are quite popular, but there are not too many streamers at the time, then you'll be the #30/#40 down the page. If you start with LoL: you are the #1000 stream.

135. Less popular – less competition

Games that are ranked lower in twitch's game list generally have fewer streamers and therefore are more approachable. Smaller communities don't necessarily mean fewer eyeballs. The Binding of Isaac was a niche game before it became popular, yet there were a thousand viewers to be gained at less competition. Similar story with TFL.

136. Bring something new into the game

If you can break up the usual gameplay with some new mechanics, then by all means – do it! Speedruns, challenges, modding, glitching, finding new ways to accomplish tasks in a game make for an interesting choice. **Lobosjr** started small, but when he began doing Dark Souls challenge runs his channel exploded!

137. Drop the games you don't like

Don't feel obligated to play a particular game. If you don't like a game or grow tired of it, then switch it and embrace a new world.

Bonus

138. Become a legend

Find a game with a relatively small (the number you're comfortable with) community and become a living legend of the game: learn its mechanics, engage in the forums, create a mod, start a wiki and draw the people to your stream. Dedicated streamers are endorsed by gaming companies and get involved in the developing process.

MFPallyTime began playing Heroes of the Storm when it was in closed beta and invested a lot of time learning and working on his mechanics. Not quite a legend yet, but a well known and fun HotS player with tons of "How To" videos. His channel has been growing exponentially since he started his HotS career.

Every time he is recording a new HotS session, he explains the abilities of the heroes he plays – every time, for the 100th time.

This is something that I miss when **Northernlion** is playing The Binding of Isaac. When he picks up a new item, that doesn't have an obvious impact on his character he just moves on, which is fine, but obviously many viewers (myself included) would enjoy a short explanation of the item's abilities and what effect it is going to have on the game.

This is something that one might expect (in a good way) from somebody who has such a big impact on the community.

139. Games on Sale

A reduced price can spark a new interest in a game and people will come to your channel to see if it is worth buying. Be sure to adjust your streaming title accordingly ("On Sale in Steam", "Worth Buying?") and give people that enter your channel a warm welcome.

Be sure to answer their questions and share your opinion about the game.

Check out Steam, GOG, Humble Bundle, Playstation and XBOX online stores or Gamersgate. Websites like isthereanydeal.com provide an aggregated view of the different shops.

140. Cater to the demand

Do some research on games you enjoy playing. If there are some bigger streamers playing that game and there is a small amount of total streams, then stream along with them. When their stream ends, their viewers will look for other streamers that play their favorite game and you will end up getting the viewers.

Reach out to the streamers and ask them about trading each other's audiences. Another thing is when the other streamer can't keep the audience entertained, people thirsting for gameplay of that game will naturally flow to your channel.

141. Analytics

Analyze the viewer/follower data after streaming a particular game, especially when you had some spikes in viewer/follower numbers. What game made the (positive) impact? Did you do something differently? Draw conclusions respectively for choosing your next game and behavior.

9. Tech and Quality Image

The way your stream looks is definitely not the most important part of your show, because it is the entertainment value that makes or breaks your stream. However, it is the first thing a new user sees when coming to your channel.

The looks and quality of your stream is something that you can control and don't have to rely on luck, fate or the Gods of Walhalla. The better the overall quality of your stream the higher are your chances to keep the viewers.

That said, a medium quality image is good enough. Good enough to start. You don't have to break the bank, immediately going out to buy all the shiny equipment, but you should work towards delivering the best image and sound possible, because, like already said before: this is something you CAN control.

There are many guides regarding hardware and software requirements for Twitch streaming, so we won't be diving too deep into this topic here and state the basics. For more guides check out the Streamer FAQs on the Twitch subreddit.

142. Streaming quality

Provide quality levels that will satisfy PC users and people that watch your stream on their mobile devices. 720p is a good choice nowadays, as it provides a clear image on normal monitors, but also caters to mobile viewers.

Whereas 360p might suit many mobile devices, it will make your stream almost impossible to enjoy for an average PC/TV user, unless you are playing Super Mario on your 8bit.

143. Frame rate

60fps is the go-to frame rate, as it shows off a very fluid and nice gameplay, especially in fast paced games, like almost every FPS.

144. Bitrate

You need to go with 2100kbps on OBS. If you set it any lower, than the stream becomes very pixelated, while setting it too high makes it "so good quality" that it becomes choppy and freezes every now and then.

New streamers having a 10mb/s upload speed and using 5k kbps make it nearly impossible to watch the stream on a mobile device, because these devices can't handle the data, even if they have a good internet connection.

145. Overall sound

Sound quality should be clear, without static or distracting background noises. Make sure your viewers tell you about any issues with the sound.

146. Game sound

Your game should be audible, but not louder than your own voice.

147. Mic

If your audio levels are not matched well or your radio is playing over your mic, then your viewers' ears will not allow them to stay for very long to listen to your cast. The chat is a good tool in this situation as well: people might give you hints about your sound levels, whether your mic is muted or echoing.

148. Internet

2-2.5 Mb upload is enough for a decent stream in 720p. More upstream would be safer and with less upload you'll need to tweak your settings to get it right. Try the following if you are stuck with slow 1MB internet:

- Lower your resolution to 480p and the framerate to 25-30

- Set your upload to 800 kbps

- Bitrate and buffer size to 700-800

- Play with the resolution downscale turning it to 1.75

- Stream classic games: NES, SNES, Genesis, Indie

10. Other Factors

You've probably heard of the short attention span of an average internet user. You need to stand out of the mass to catch their attention and to make that average user click on your stream.

Having a nice and clean structure, as well as some custom graphics won't instantly lure thousands of viewers to your channel, but it will have an impact in the long run.

The title and the overlays are the only things besides game screenshot and viewers that are visible to the potential viewer while browsing the game directory. And the best thing – as opposed to both other factors you have the control over your titles and overlays! Make sure you make them appealing.

10.1 Channel Page Design

Not everybody is an artist or a web designer. We are all here just to play some games for entertainment, right? Right, but making your channel stand out with pretty visuals and important information is not that hard or time-consuming as you might think.

149. Invest in some visuals in general

You don't have to be an artist yourself. In case you have missed it at the beginning of this book: I have prepared a special gift for the buyers of this book, called **"10 Easy Steps To A Professional Twitch Overlay For FREE!"**

In this free guide you will learn how you can get beautifully and professionally designed Twitch overlays, banners or avatars for you channel for free! You can download it following this link:

http://www.streamingmentality.com/stream-smarter

This is my way of saying *Thank You* for buying this book.

These visuals will make a better first impression and tell first-time visitors that you are committed to Twitch.

150. Have a descriptive overlay for different scenes

You want them to be eye-catching and self-explanatory, so when a new user shows up they'll know immediately what the channel is about and what to do next: when you are streaming, AFK, offline, etc.

A pretty, branded image is nice, but it also needs to be descriptive if you want to capture the viewer's attention: the games you're playing, ways to connect with you via social media when you're offline, etc.

Good examples:

- **Lobosjr** and his offline screen: displaying the stream schedule, games played and social media directions;

- **Jooygirl**: clean, simple and entertaining, showing off the Twitter account as the main way to connect.

Bad examples:

- twitter.com/badlayouts. Don't forget that the stream is still about the game as well.

151. The About area

Your "About" panel is one of the most important ones, if not the most important panel on your channel. Use it to tell a few things about you, but more importantly what a viewer will be getting out of your stream.

Most people that stumble upon your channel do not really care what your favorite color is or that you call your dog Heisenberg.

What they really want to know is:

- What are the benefits of watching your channel?

- Why should they stay?

- Etc.

Be sure to make it apparent for them, saying what you'll be streaming and why you are the best choice.

152. Share your schedule and gaming playlist

This gives your viewers something to look forward to. Even if they don't like some parts of your show of certain games, they will tune in for the other.

153. Make it easy to stay in touch with you

Share your contact and social media information (Facebook, Twitter, Youtube) and other non-Twitch platforms. Make some personal information, like age and e-mail available, as well as your homepage and the best ways to get in contact with you.

154. Include your details

If you upload your games to other platforms like YouTube, you want your overlays to have a link to your Twitch channel. The YouTube visitor will want to check out your Twitch channel as well.

155. Set some rules

If you don't, your chat will fill up with trolls that scare away the townsfolk that will be gone for good. Write down the rules in your channel description, but give your followers some room to breathe. You might want to consider setting some restrictions around the usual suspects: sports, politics, religion and international affairs.

156. Hall of Fame

Give your top supporters and favorite broadcasters a special treatment on your channel's page. It gives the people a section of fame on your board and other viewers an obligation for aspiration.

10.2 Stream Titles

Make your titles look interesting, unique, descriptive and exciting. All other things being equal people are more likely to join a stream featuring energetic titles. If they see somebody who is having "Meh…" as the stream's title, they'll probably go to "No death challenge, all% - Watch me win!" instead.

157. First things first

Put the most important information or hook in the beginning:

- Speedrun,

- Co-Op,

- Day/Episode

- Blind Playthrough,

- Ranked,

- Region/Server for MOBA/MMO,

- Subs Match.

158. Be concise

Clearly label in the title what the current show is about; down to the level, map and mode: "Hardmode on Barb - Diablo 3", "Destro Lock PvP 3vs3 3k Rating - WoW", "Mundo Top Lane Random Queue LoL". And don't forget to sync the title for the game with the actual game you're playing.

159. Include your resolution/framerate

If people are looking for a particular resolution, they might check you out:

- Low - for mobile devices

- High – for watching your stream on a big HDTV

160. Put the name of the game at the end of the title

Although the Twitch browse view will show the game you are playing; this is meant for the e-mail notification for your followers when you go live. This way they see what game you are playing.

161. End the title with a pun or funny

Funny and interesting titles are harder to come by, but they are worth it.

11. Setting Goals and Taking Action

You need to have a growth strategy based on what you read here, as well as to know and to write down what your main goal is: to live off Twitch streaming, to have 1,000 followers, to become a partner, to raise money for charity, etc.

162. Setting smaller goals

Split that main goal into step stones that you need to accomplish in order to get to that end goal. The step stones can and should be split into even smaller goals on your way to the big pie.

163. Taking action

Having a goal is important, but having a system that works for you is even more important. The "Focusing Question" from Gary Keller's book "The ONE Thing" can help establishing your goals and a system to achieve them.

Example:

To help breaking down your goals, ask yourself the Focusing Question: *"What is the single most important thing I can achieve **someday** on Twitch, such that by doing it EVERYTHING else in my life becomes easier or unnecessary?"*

Answer: Live off Twitch streaming.

Then ask yourself yet another question: *"What is the single most important thing I can do **this year** to live off Twitch Streaming someday?"*

Answer: Get over 500 subscribers.

Q: *"What is the single most important thing I can do **in the next 6 months** to live off Twitch Streaming someday?"*

Answer: Stream 5 days per week consistently.

Q: *"What is the single most important thing I can do **in the next 2 months** to live off Twitch Streaming someday?"*

Answer: Become part of a major team streaming Game X.

Q: *"What is the single most important thing I can do **next month** to live off Twitch Streaming someday?"*

Answer: Establish myself as an expert on Game X.

Q: *"What is the single most important thing I can do **next week** to live off Twitch Streaming someday?"*

Answer: Host a tournament with 4 other streamers.

Q: *"What is the single most important thing I can do **tomorrow** to live off Twitch Streaming someday?"*

Answer: Run some tests to have a better streaming image quality.

Q: *"What is the single most important thing I can do **today** to live off Twitch Streaming someday?"*

Answer: Ask 20 fellow streamers from niche about a collaborative event.

Q: *"What is the single most important thing I can do **right now** to live off Twitch Streaming someday?"*

Answer: Stream!

You can grab a copy "The ONE Thing" by Gary Keller to learn more about the ONE thing and the focusing question. The essence of it boils down to start asking yourself a broad focusing question and narrowing it down to the point of what you can do right now to achieve your main goal. You can ask the focusing question about any goal in any area of your life.

To get to your goals you need to set up corresponding habits and then work hard to achieve them. Measure the impact of your actions, adapt your strategy and tick off things off your to-do list.

Sample goals:

164. Monthly goals

- streaming X times a week,

- never miss a streaming day,

- Get X new followers

165. Weekly goals

- say "hello" to 20 other streamers from a similar niche,

- reach out to 10 streamers about a collaborative stream,

- write 20 useful forum posts on your favorite gaming forum,

- create 2 relevant blog posts on a subreddit of your favorite game,

- retweet/comment daily on Social Media of your favorite streamer.

166. Daily goals

- gain a level on the game you're streaming,

- kill a boss,

- ask your viewers 5 questions.

167. Accountability

Tell viewers about your goals if you want and place them prominently on your channel page.

168. Dream big

…but be realistic about your expectations - successful streamers aren't born or made overnight, they are forged and tested over time.

169. The dark side

Twitch streamers need viewers, followers and subscribers and they are sure to try just about anything to get them. Viewer bots, buying followers and other non-compliant stuff.

Stay away from it, because sooner or later it is going to catch up with you. Famous examples are Ricegum and EggYSC2 that had been banned for viewer-botting.

170. Streaming is a marathon, not a sprint

Many streamers who are just starting out are not able to grasp what seasoned streamers learned the hard way: how patient you have to be to grow a channel. Time by itself is a secret sauce that for a change works in your favor.

In fact, it is not common to grow a big channel overnight and this is why most people tend to giving up after some time.

It is rather rare, that a new channel gains a powerful momentum, reaching thousands of viewers after a few months. Slow growth is common though and those people that persevere rip the rewards. Like a tree, your twitch channel and your own brand take time to grow.

Depending on how much effort you put into consistently supporting, cultivating and just being patient about it, it will grow either into a rich, beautiful tree or will wither before it reaches maturity.

171. NEVER GIVE UP

Time and Tenacity. That is what matters. If you are reading this all the way through, you already have the patience and the will to improve that most people lack. In the end, it is consistency and positive thinking that will triumph and help overcome all the obstacles on your way to the top.

I know you will be successful.

Afterword – Doing the Work

This book is the key to your success as a streamer on Twitch. The advantage you will receive from it will be in the exact proportion to the action it inspires in you. To benefit from it you don't have to agree with every single statement made here. But many aspects of streaming on Twitch.tv described in this book will hopefully strike the right chord.

You have to actively get new viewers, not leaving it to chance.

The magic bullet does not exist.

Do the work.

It is important to get the initial followers and keep the ball rolling thereafter. You need viewers to get viewers – sad, but true. This is the so-called snowball effect.

More viewers equal a higher chance of getting followers. More followers generally mean a better chance that some of these followers tune in when you stream which will push your live stream to the top of the Twitch ranking.

And this fact will get you more viewers and more potential followers to magnify the effect even more in return. Middle to long term the snowball effect will make you stumble up the Twitch ladder effectively, gaining a larger following almost by the hour when you stream.

If you are serious about Twitch streaming and you put in the work – I guarantee you that you will see the results, that's how it works.

But you need to have a goal for yourself and take action towards reaching it using the advice given in this book. Every time you want to take your channel one step further or things aren't going according to plan and you find yourself wanting to quit and join the 99.9% one inch short before striking gold – here is a solution for you in 3 easy steps:

1. Go back to the very beginning of this book and reread the intro chapter

2. Reread the rest

3. **APPLY** the advice on these pages and write me an e-mail if you have any questions (streamingmentality@gmail.com)

Assess your channel and stream in accordance to the presented guidelines. I can't stress this enough – ideas and knowledge aren't worth much without execution. You will start gaining momentum after you actually *start USING* the advice described in this guide step by step.

Don't let fears or uncertainty paralyze you, if you've set yourself a goal, move towards that goal every day, no matter what. A journey of a thousand miles begins with a single step – one single step every day will eventually get you to that goal.

About the Author

I am passionate about games. Putting this guide together was a lot of work and a great personal accomplishment for me. I hope that this book will give your Twitch channel the much deserved boost, as well as provide the help and guidance necessary to reach your goals. May your channel live long and prosper.

THANK YOU FOR BUYING THIS BOOK

I would love to hear your thoughts! While it's easy to connect over Social Media, it is often better to have one-on-one conversations with readers like you.

If you have any questions, suggestions or just want to say hi, write me an e-mail here: streamingmentality@gmail.com.

For more guides, information about streaming and gaming in general, please visit http://www.streamingmentality.com.

If this book has helped you, please consider leaving a review an Amazon.

Below, I would like to thank these community giants for their awesome work, helpful advice and inspiration! In alphabetical order:

Aremis86

Bananasaurus_Rex

BroBQ

Buffet_Time

Cem0re

Dansgaming

Darkwinge

DjQuad

Ferretbomb

Geekyantics

Hlswaglord

Jooygirl

Livinpink

Lobosjr

Lockzhere

ManVsGame

Markiplier

MFPallyTime

MissMiaRose

Ms_Vixen

Nobbel87

Northernlion

Obezianka

OneRandomDolly

OverBoredGaming

PeterCyran

PewDiePie

Pinworms666

ProHenis

ShannaNina

SilentSentry

Sky_mp3

Swifty

TaraBabcock

TheOddOne

ThunderCast

Towelliee

TrumpSC

TSM_Dyrus

veeBunni

VoiceOfKarnage

WKJezz

... and everyone else who helped in creating this resource for streamers.

12958497R00049

Printed in Great Britain
by Amazon